THE CATHOLIC MASS BOOKLET FOR KIDS

How to use this book:

Your child can use this book as a coloring book or they can simply use it to follow along with the Mass.

Use the signs on each page to know when to sit, stand, or kneel.

The child can follow along with each stepping stone. Each step brings us closer to the end of Mass, but more importantly, closer to God.

The Mass brings us closer to God.

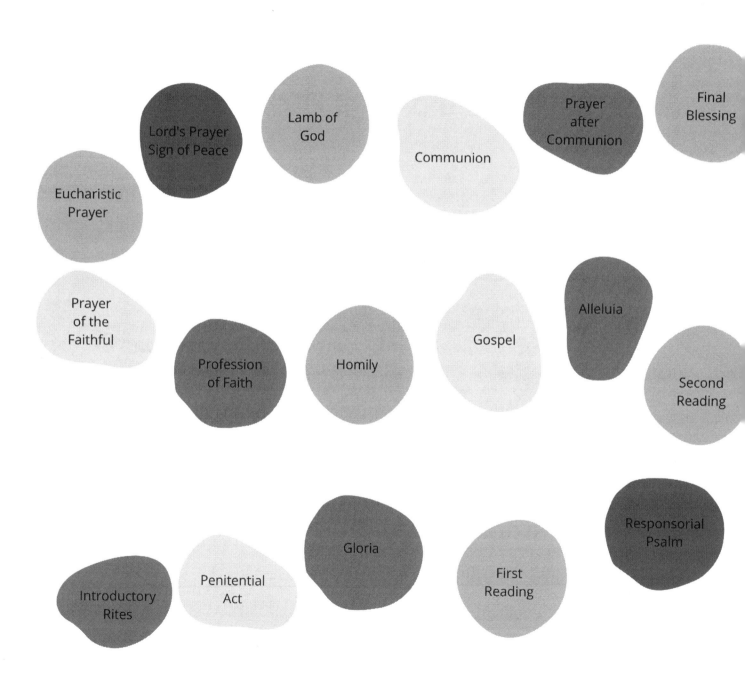

Welcome to Church, the
HOUSE of GOD

In church, I can be:

QUIET

RESPECTFUL

ATTENTIVE

OPEN

LOVING

HOPEFUL

GRATEFUL

Dip your
fingers in
HOLY WATER

MAKE THE

Touch your
forehead

Touch your
chest

SIGN of the CROSS

Touch your left shoulder

Touch your right shoulder

GENUFLECT

at the pew

I SPY

Crucifix

Bible

Candles

Pew

Stand for the
PROCESSION

The priest says:

In the name of the FATHER, and of the SON, and of the HOLY SPIRIT

We say:

AMEN

The priest says:

The LORD be with you.

We respond with:

And with your spirit.

Penitential Act

I confess to almighty God
and to you, my brothers and sisters,
that I have greatly sinned,
in my thoughts and in my words,
in what I have done and in what I have
failed to do,
through my fault, through my fault,
through my most grievous fault;
therefore I ask blessed Mary ever-Virgin,
all the Angels and Saints,
and you, my brothers and sisters,
to pray for me to the Lord our God.

For the first and second reading
The lector says:

The WORD of the LORD.

We respond with:

Thanks be to GOD.

LITERGY of the WORD

We sit and listen to the

first reading

PSALM

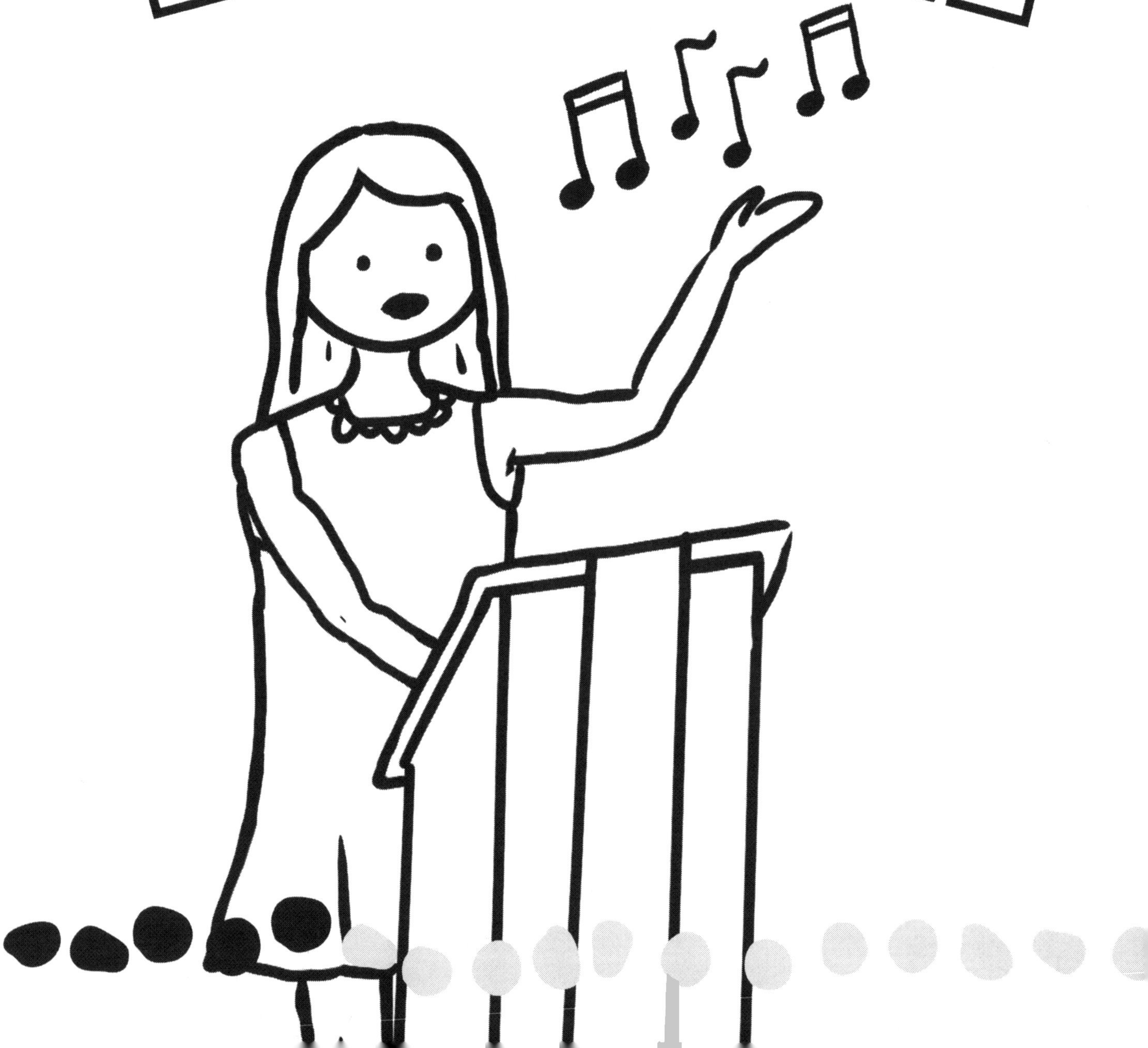

We sit and listen to the
second reading

Before the GOSPEL:
The priest or deacon says:
The LORD be with you.

We respond with
And with your SPIRIT.

The priest or deacon says:
A reading from the HOLY GOSPEL according to [Matthew, Mark, Luke, John].

We respond with
GLORY to your O LORD.

Stand for the Alleluia and the GOSPEL

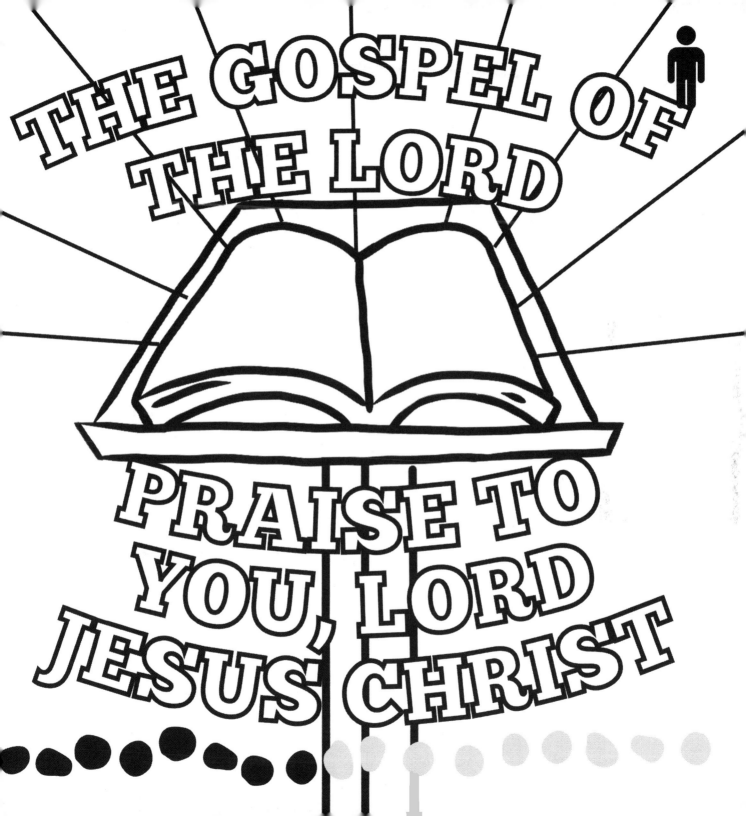

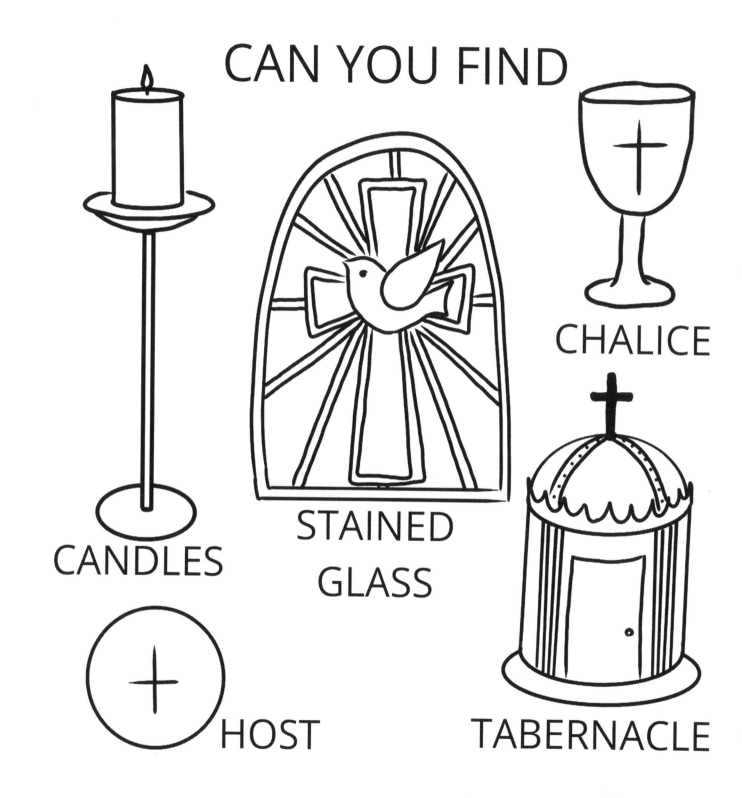

CAN YOU FIND

CHALICE

CANDLES

STAINED
GLASS

HOST

TABERNACLE

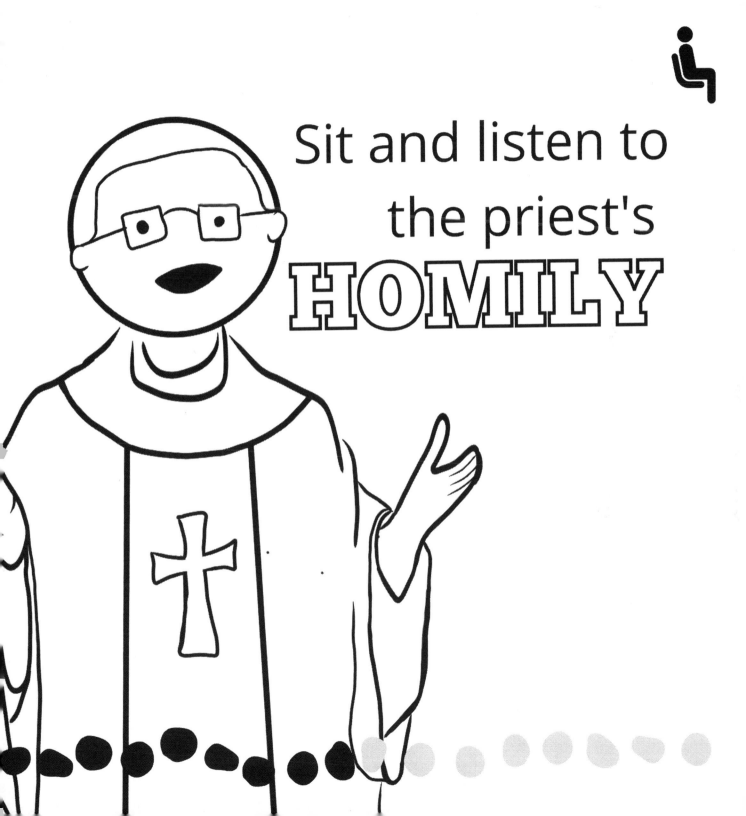

Sit and listen to the priest's **HOMILY**

Profession of Faith
Nicene Creed

I believe in one God, the Father Almighty,
maker of heaven and earth,
of all things visible and invisible.

I believe in one Lord Jesus Christ,
the Only Begotten Son of God,
born of the Father before all ages.
God from God, Light from Light,
true God from true God,
begotten, not made, consubstantial with
the Father;
through Him all things were made.
For us men and for our salvation He came
down from heaven,
and by the Holy Spirit was incarnate of the
Virgin Mary,
and became man.

For our sake He was crucified under
Pontius Pilate,
He suffered death and was buried,
and rose again on the third day
in accordance with the Scriptures.

He ascended into heaven
and is seated at the right hand of the
Father.
He will come again in glory
to judge the living and the dead
and His kingdom will have no end.

I believe in the Holy Spirit,
the Lord, the giver of life,
who proceeds from the Father and the
Son,
who with the Father and the Son is
adored and glorified,
who has spoken through the prophets.

I believe in one, holy, catholic and
apostolic Church.
I confess one Baptism for the
forgiveness of sins
and I look forward to the resurrection o
the dead
and the life of the world to come.
Amen.

Profession of Faith

Apostles Creed
I believe in God,
the Father Almighty,
Creator of heaven and earth,
and in Jesus Christ, His only Son, our Lord,
who was conceived by the Holy Spirit,
born of the Virgin Mary,
suffered under Pontius Pilate,
was crucified, died and was buried;
He descended into hell;
on the third day He rose again from the dead;
He ascended into heaven,
and is seated at the right hand of God the Father Almighty;
from there He will come to judge the living and the dead.
I believe in the Holy Spirit,
the holy catholic Church,
the communion of saints,
the forgiveness of sins,
the resurrection of the body,
and life everlasting.
Amen.

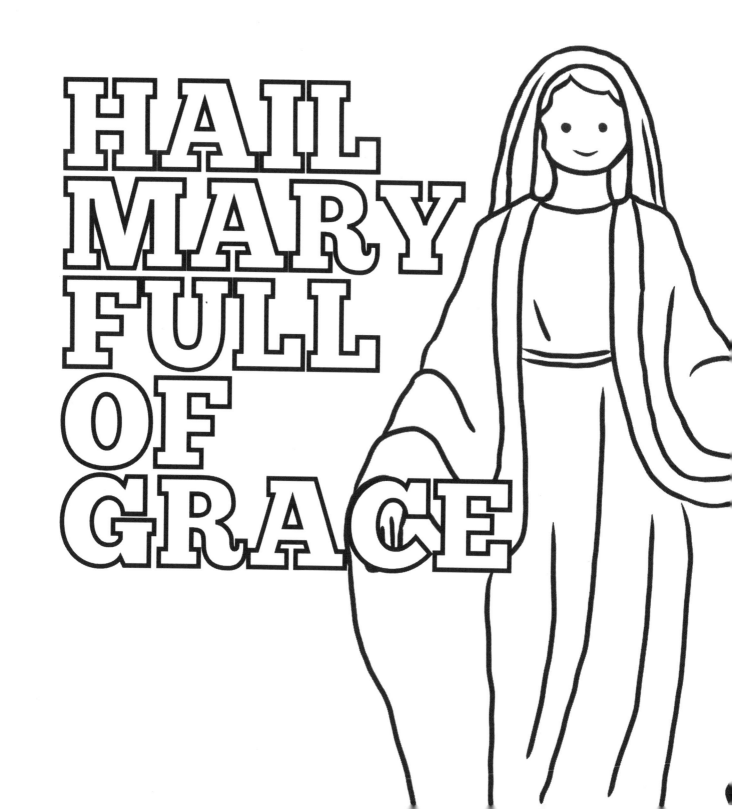

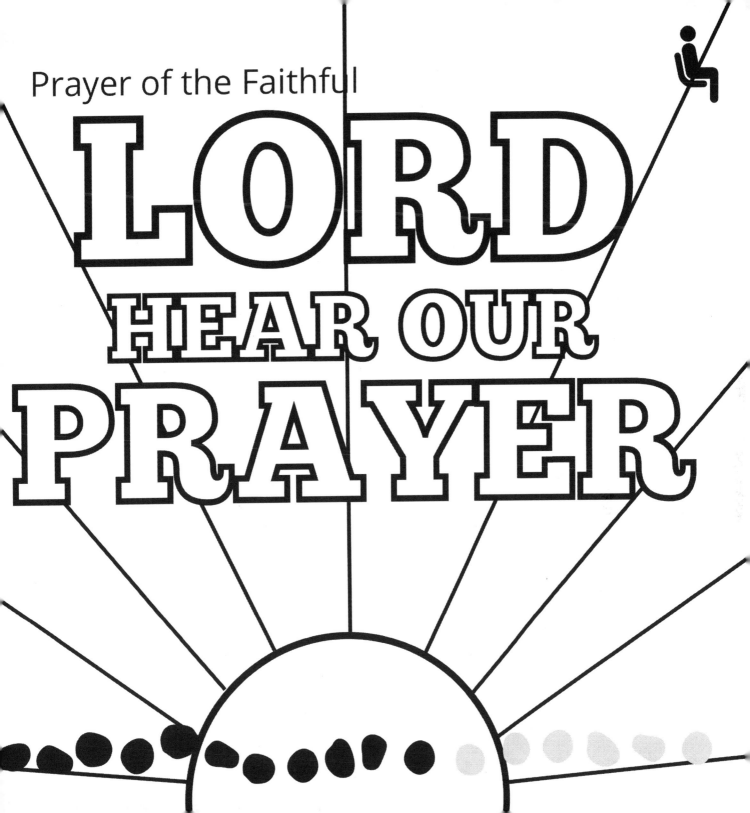

Prayer of the Faithful

LORD
HEAR OUR
PRAYER

The Litergy of the Eucharist

The priest says:

Pray, brethren (brothers and sisters), that my sacrifice and yours may be acceptable to God, the almighty Father.

We all say:

May the Lord accept the sacrifice at your hands for the praise and glory of His name, for our good and the good of all his holy Church.

Eucharistic Prayer

The priest says:
The LORD be with you.

We respond with
And with your SPIRIT.

The priest says:
Lift up your hearts.

We respond with
We lift them up to the LORD.

The priest says:
Let us give thanks to the LORD our GOD.

We respond with
It is RIGHT and JUST.

The MYSTERY of FAITH

As we proclaim your death, O LORD and profess your Resurection, until you come again.

The LORD'S Prayer

OUR FATHER
who art in **HEAVEN**
hallowed be Thy name
Thy **KINGDOM** come
Thy will be done
on earth as it is in **HEAVEN**
give us this day
our daily bread
and **FORGIVE US**
as we forgive those who
trespass against us
and lead us not into
temptation but deliver
us from evil.

The priest says:

The peace of the LORD be with you always.

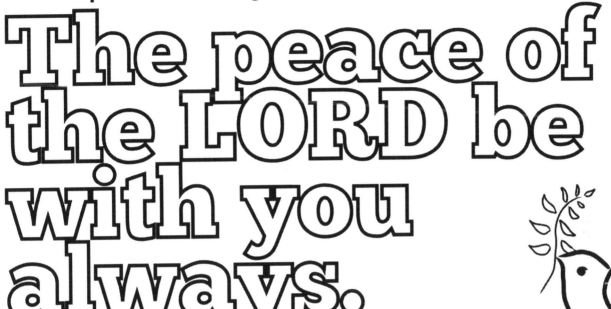

We respond with:

And with your spirit.

LAMB of GOD
you take away the sins of the world, have mercy on us.

LAMB of GOD
you take away the sins of the world, have mercy on us.

LAMB of GOD
you take away the sins of the world, grant us peace.

INVITATION to COMMUNION

The priest says:
Behold the Lamb of God, behold him who takes away the sins of the world. Blessed are those called to the supper of the lamb.

We all say:
Lord, I am not worthy that you should enter under my roof, but only say the word and my soul shall be healed.

BEHOLD the LAMB of GOD

CONCLUDING RITES

The priest says:
The LORD be with you.

We respond with
And with your SPIRIT.

The priest says:
Go forth, the Mass has ended.

We respond with
Thanks be to GOD.

Made in the USA
Columbia, SC
08 November 2024

46033568R00026